EARLY ELEMENTARY

TAKE A BOW!

8 SPARKLING PIANO SOLOS

BOOK 1

GREAT RECITAL PIECES!

BY CAROLYN MILLER

ISBN 978-1-61774-264-4

WILLIS MUSIC

EXCLUSIVELY DISTRIBUTED BY

HAL•LEONARD®
CORPORATION
7777 W. BLUEMOUND RD. P.O. BOX 13819 MILWAUKEE, WI 53213

Visit Hal Leonard Online at
www.halleonard.com

FROM THE COMPOSER

Recital time is a happy time! I believe that the recital solo should be carefully chosen to give each student the best chance for success in front of an unfamiliar audience. It is my hope that students will master the carefully selected solos in this book so that a winning performance takes place.

I have included a variety of pieces: many are energetic, dance-like solos with fun lyrics to sing along with, like "Clap Hands Dance" and "Barnyard Boogie"; others explore the different sounds the piano is capable of making, like the sound of bells in "Big Ben." Another personal favorite is "Tico Taco," which aids rhythmic skills. Optional teacher accompaniments have also been included to give students the opportunity to gain valuable skills needed for future ensemble playing.

My wish is that these pieces will entertain as well as motivate students of any age.

Please enjoy!

Carolyn Miller

CONTENTS

Clap Hands Dance

Words and Music by
Carolyn Miller

Lively

Let your hands go clap, clap. Let your fin - gers snap, snap.

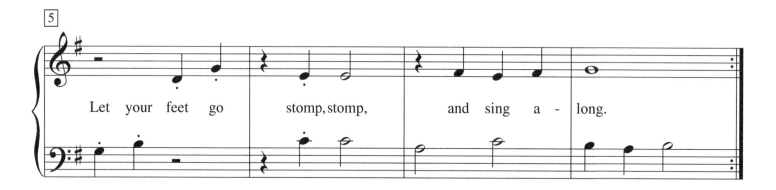

Let your feet go stomp, stomp, and sing a - long.

We are sing - ing, we are danc - ing, we are hav - ing lots of fun.

Accompaniment (Student plays as written.)

Lively

Sing a Happy Song

Words and Music by
Carolyn Miller

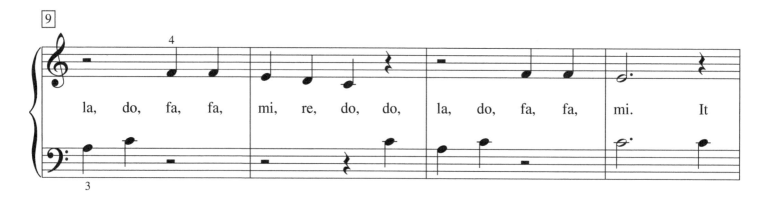

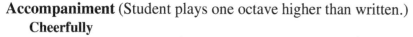

Accompaniment (Student plays one octave higher than written.)

Big Ben

Arranged by
Carolyn Miller

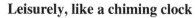

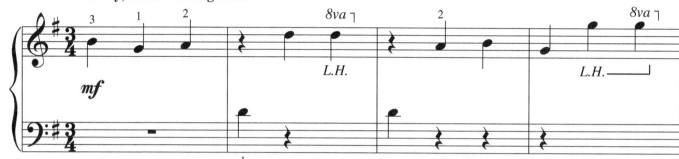

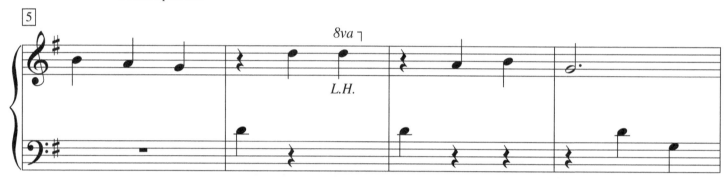

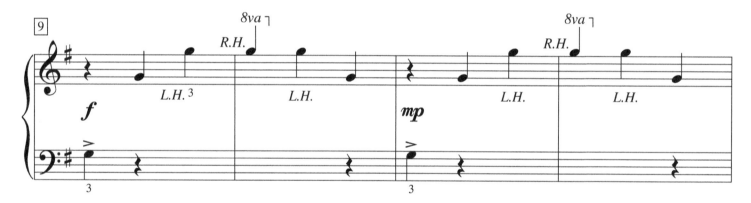

Accompaniment (Student plays one octave higher than written.)

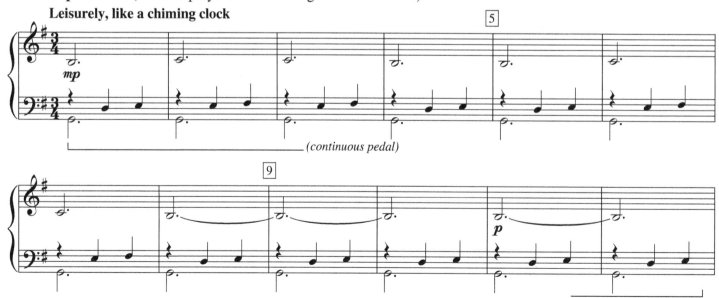

9

The Curious Kitten

Carolyn Miller

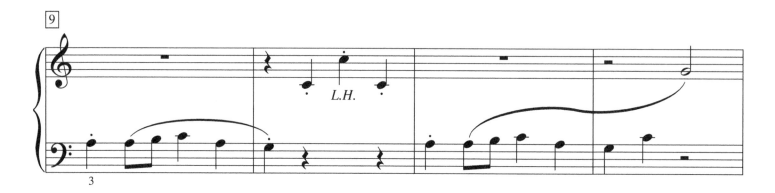

Accompaniment (Student plays one octave higher than written.)

Hoedown

Words and Music by
Carolyn Miller

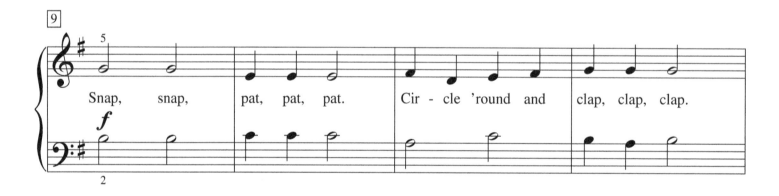

Snap, snap, pat, pat, pat. Cir-cle 'round and clap, clap, clap.

Accompaniment (Student plays one octave higher than written.)

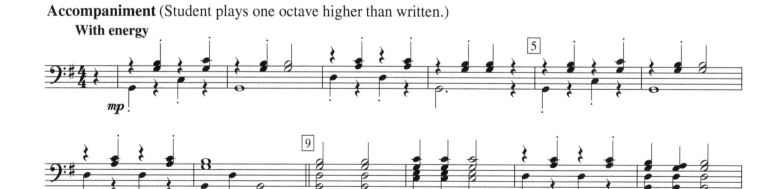

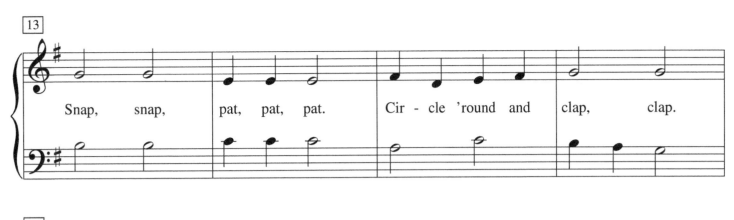

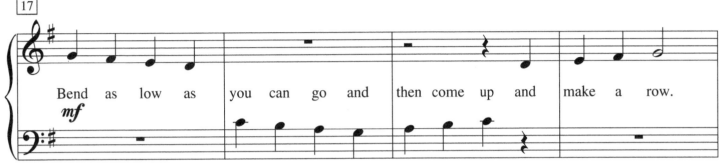

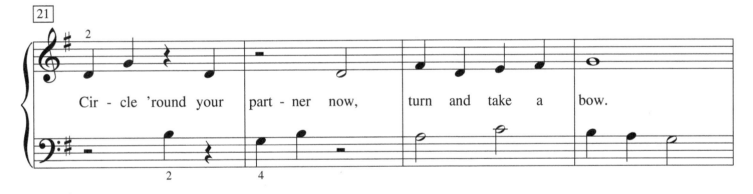

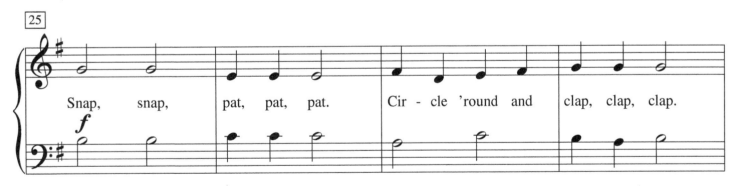

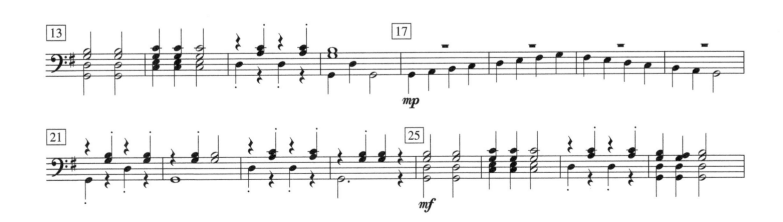

Snap,   snap,   pat, pat, pat.   Cir - cle 'round and   clap!

Tico Taco

Words and Music by
Carolyn Miller

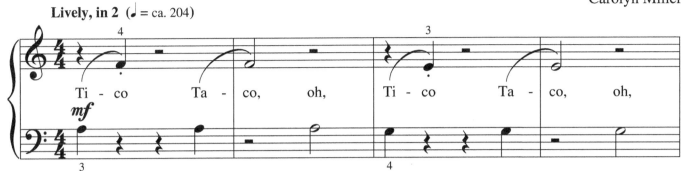

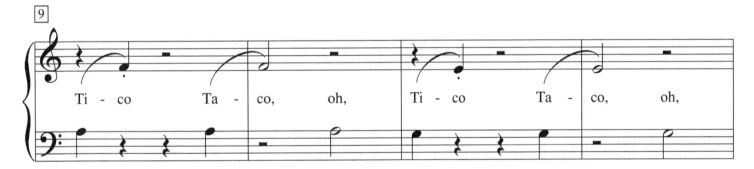

Ti - co Ta - co, oh, Ti - co Ta - co, oh,

Ti - co Ta - co, it is such fun to sing this song.

Ti - co Ta - co, oh, Ti - co Ta - co, oh,

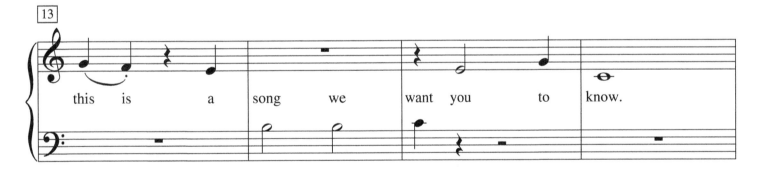

this is a song we want you to know.

Accompaniment (Student plays one octave higher than written.)

Lively, in 2 (♩ = ca. 204)

We love to sing___ and dance and twirl all a - round___ and then we

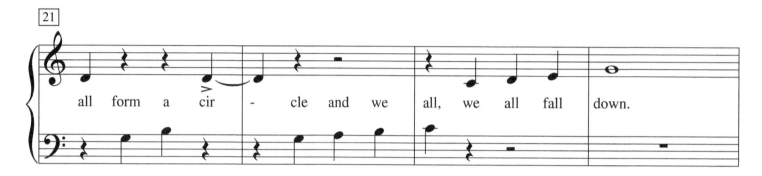

all form a cir - cle and we all, we all fall down.

We get up quick - ly and then cir - cle a - gain___ un - til the

lead - er calls out___ to all: "This is the end!"

This is a song we want you all to know!

Barnyard Boogie

Words and Music by
Carolyn Miller

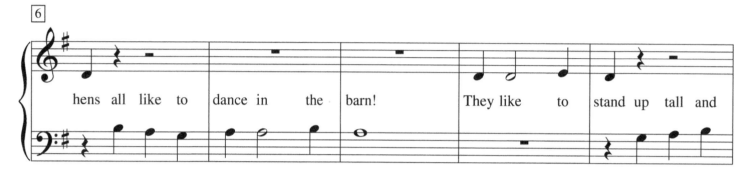

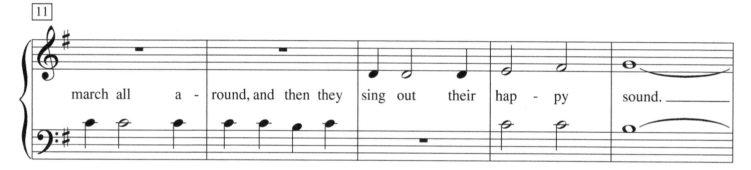

Accompaniment (Student plays one octave higher than written.)

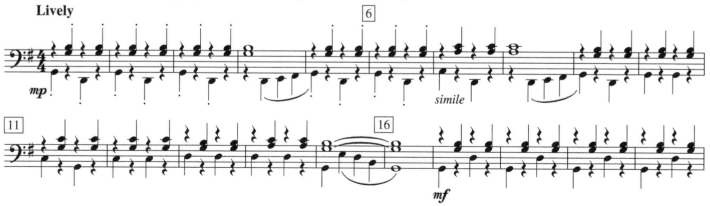

Watch them do the barn-yard boo - gie, watch them do the

barn-yard dance! Swing and sway, and come on now, just take a chance!

Swing it, sway it, barn-yard boo - gie is the dance! *f* (Dance!)

The Merry-Go-Round

Words and Music by
Carolyn Miller

Accompaniment (Student plays one octave higher than written.)

ABOUT THE COMPOSER

Carolyn Miller's teaching and composing career spans over 40 prolific years. She graduated with honors from the College Conservatory of Music at the University of Cincinnati with a degree in music education, and later earned a masters degree in elementary education from Xavier University. Carolyn regularly presents workshops throughout the United States and is a frequent adjudicator at festivals and competitions. Although she recently retired from the Ohio public school system, she continues to maintain her own private studio.

Carolyn's music emphasizes essential technical skills, is remarkably fun to play, and appeals to both children and adults. Well-known television personality Regis Philbin performed her pieces "Rolling River" and "Fireflies" in 1992 and 1993 on national television. Carolyn's compositions appear frequently on state contest lists, including the NFMC Festivals Bulletin. She is listed in the *Who's Who in America* and *Who's Who in American Women*.

In her spare time Carolyn directs the Northminster Presbyterian Church Choir in Cincinnati, Ohio and enjoys spending time with her family, especially her seven grandchildren.